J.C. 8⁰⁰

op

The Ox . . .
The Ass . . .
The Oyster . . .

Edited by HENRY and MARIE EINSPRUCH

THE LEWIS AND HARRIET LEDERER FOUNDATION
6204 Park Heights Avenue   Baltimore, Maryland 21215

ACKNOWLEDGMENTS

Second Edition
Copyright © 1975 by Henry and Marie Einspruch
Library of Congress Catalog Card Number: 74-25243
Printed in the U.S.A.

Christianity Has Not Failed; It Has Not Been Tried by Dr. Russell Kirk. Copyright, General Features Corporation. Reprinted by permission

Israel's Peculiar Position reprinted by permission of Eric Hoffer.

Jacob's Ladder reprinted by permission of Fred Kendal.

"Joy Cometh in the Morning" by Rachmiel Frydland. From the publication of the same name. Reprinted by permission of Beth Sar Shalom, Toronto.

My Daughter and the Sphinx reprinted by permission of Moishe Rosen.

There Are Two Seas in Israel by Bruce Barton. Reprinted by permission of the Executors of the Estate of Randall Barton.

Who's Who gives a brief biography of some of the writers.

Illustrations:

Cover Page drawn by Muriel Einspruch Hopkins
Broadsides drawn by Steffi Geiser Rubin
Drawings by E. M. Lilien

All unsigned articles are from the pen of the editors.
Words which have a * are listed in a **Glossary.**

CONTENTS

Introduction

The material in this book has had a checkered career. Most of it has been presented in Yiddish over the radio; some of it is a condensation of talks given over the years; and a number of the articles are based on material which has appeared in various publications, to which due credit is given.

A minimum of editing has been done in order to preserve the oral quality of speaking, for these messages were meant to be heard, rather than read.

This book is presented in the hope that it will challenge the reader to compare the mundane, materialistic things of everyday life, with the world of truth, justice, love, judgment, and forgiveness.

The quality of the present NOW depends not only on the things of today, but also on what the future holds for us.

Perhaps these messages will lead the way.

The Editors

.

The Ox . . .

The Ass . . .

The Oyster . . .

The gypsy has no mission in life other than to tell fortunes and roam over the face of the globe, and the fortunes he tells are invariably those of other people, and not his own. He seldom settles down, nor does he become involved in the problems or conditions of the community in which he happens to find himself. That is why a gypsy is a gypsy.

It never occurs to any people on the face of the earth, other than to the Jew, to question their mission in life, and to be concerned as to whether or not they are carrying it out.

The probabilities are that the ancestors of the Jews did not attempt to justify their presence among men, nor even dream of a purpose in life that would justify their existence. Neither does the ox in his stall, nor the ass in the field, nor the oyster in his bed question themselves as to what service they owe to humanity; it is sufficient for them that they exist.

But let a people like us Jews exist, despite every effort to destroy us, and we must explain our continued existence to ourselves and our miraculous persistence to the world-at-large.

1

Historians generally find themselves at a loss to explain the Jewish existence, and in Mark Twain's essay, "Concerning the Jews," he has this to say:

"If statistics are right, the Jews constitute but one percent of the human race. It suggests a nebulous dim puff of star dust lost in the blaze of the Milky Way. Properly the Jew ought hardly to be heard of; but he is heard of, has always been heard of. He is as prominent on the planet as any other people, and his commercial importance is extravagantly out of proportion to the smallness of his bulk.

"His contributions to the world's list of great names in literature, science, art, music, finance, medicine, and abstruse learning are also away out of proportion to the weakness of his numbers. He has made a marvelous fight in this world, in all the ages; and has done it with his hands tied behind him.

"He could be vain of himself, and be excused for it. The Egyptian, the Babylonian, and the Persian rose, filled the planet with sound and splendor, then faded to dream-stuff and passed away; the Greek and the Roman followed, and made a vast noise, and they are gone; other peoples have sprung up and held their torch high for a time, but it burned out, and they sit in twilight now, or have vanished.

"The Jew saw them all, beat them all, and is now what he always was, exhibiting no decadence, no infirmities of age, no weakening of his parts, no slowing of his energies, no dulling of his alert and aggressive mind. All things are mortal but the Jew; all other forces pass, but he remains.

"What is the secret of his immortality?"

It must be apparent to the more serious among us, to those who have not become strangers to our divine history, to the writings of the prophets, the books of Jonah, Ruth, and those of the New Testament, that, unlike the gypsies, we were vested with a mission.

What is the mission of the Jew? To be the world's bankers? Olympic swimmers? Educators? Politicians? In the Tenach* we are called God's "witnesses." The Prophet Isaiah says, in chapter 43, verse 10: "You are my witnesses, says the Lord." But this is not our avocation. As a matter of fact, most of us pride ourselves on not being missionaries.

"This people have I formed for myself that they may show forth my glory," is one of a host of affirmations by the prophets (Isaiah 43:20), and in the New Testament we read that the Messiah Jesus commissioned his Jewish disciples to "Go into all the world and preach the Gospel—the good news of God—to every creature." (Mark 16:15)

Every once in a while our rabbis orate on the mission of Judaism, contending that the purpose of our dispersion was to bring a knowledge of the true God to the peoples of the earth. But are we actually doing anything about it?

Our reluctance to fulfill our destiny, however, did not checkmate God. What we refused to do, others have done. The God of Abraham, Isaac, and Jacob is known throughout the world today; our prophets, Moses, and the Psalms are the prized possession of the human race, not because of our efforts, but because others have done that for which we were chosen.

The pages of the New Testament teem with incidents of activity among Jews and non-Jews in the interest of the messianic movement. What today is celebrated as Pentecost in the Church is but a harking back to that memorable Shavuot* when 3,000 Jews allied themselves with the nascent movement and laid the foundation of a fellowship which has transcended race, time, and clime.

Inspired by the Messiah Jesus they carried the Torah* and the prophetic teachings beyond the confines of school and Temple, to bring countless myriads under the wings of the Shekinah glory.

Among those in the front ranks have been men of our own race. The list is long, we mention but a few.

Who has not heard of Samuel Isaac Joseph Schereschewsky, the Lithuanian Jew, who went to Shanghai and translated the entire Bible into Mandarin and Wenli.

And what about Isidor Loewenthal, born an Orthodox Jew in Prussian Poland, who went to Afghanistan and, before his untimely death at the age of thirty-seven, completed a manuscript of a dictionary, as well as a translation of the New Testament into Pushtu, the common language of the people.

Dr. Bernard Bettelheim was the first Protestant missionary to Japan. A Hungarian Jew, talented linguist, he made the first translation of parts of the Bible into Chinese and Japanese, and also compiled a Japanese grammar and dictionary. Fifty-seven years after his death a monument was erected to him in Ryuku, Japan, in recognition of his contribution as physician, translator, and teacher.

It is, of course, within our power to refuse to accept and carry out the mission for which we were destined. We can, if we choose, descend to the level of the ox, the ass, and the oyster. On the other hand, we can also rise to our predestined heights—become a messianic people, the carriers of the world's redemption.

"Israel! Arise, shine, for your Light has come." (Isaiah 60:1)

Alfred Edersheim
Says . . .

If the claims of Jesus have been rejected by the Jewish nation, he has at least fulfilled one part of the mission prophetically assigned to the Messiah.

Whether or not he be the Lion of the tribe of Judah, to him, assuredly, has been the gathering of the nations, and the isles have waited for his law. Passing the narrow bounds of obscure Judaea, and breaking down the walls of national prejudice and isolation, he has made the sublimer teaching of the Old Testament the common possession of the world, and founded a great brotherhood, of which the God of Israel is the Father.

He alone has exhibited a life in which absolutely no fault could be found; and promulgated a teaching to which absolutely no exception can be taken. Admittedly, he was the One Perfect Man—the ideal of humanity; and his teaching the one absolute teaching. The world has known none other, none equal, and the world has owned it, if not by the testimony of words, yet by the evidence of facts.

The Man of Nazareth has, by universal consent, been the mightiest Factor in our world's history: alike politically, socially, intellectually, and morally.

If Jesus be not the Messiah, he has at least thus far done the Messiah's work. If he be not the Messiah, there has at least been none other, before or after him. If he be not the Messiah, the world has not, and never can have, a Messiah. (THE LIFE AND TIMES OF JESUS THE MESSIAH, Volume I, p. 180)

IN THE OLDE DAYS WHEN AMERICA WAS BORN, THE PILGRIMS AND THE INDIANS GOT TOGETHER AND ATE TURKEY WITH DRESSING, CRANBERRY SAUCE, CORN-ON-THE-COB... AND EVERYONE GAVE THANKS BECAUSE THE HARVEST WAS ABUNDANT AND BECAUSE NOBODY GOT SCALPED AND EVERYBODY GOT FED.

THEY WERE GRATEFUL TO GOD BECAUSE THEY BELIEVED THAT ALL GOOD THINGS CAME FROM HIS MERCY.

TODAY, THANKSGIVING HAS BECOME ONE OF **america's** FAVORITE HOLIDAYS: WE EAT TURKEY WITH DRESSING, CRANBERRY SAUCE, CORN-ON-THE-COB, SWEET POTATO PIE, MINCE-MEAT PIE, PUMPKIN PIE... AND ALKA SELTZER

UGH... I CAN'T BELIEVE I ATE THE WHOLE THING

BUT HARDLY ANYBODY GIVES THANKS ALTHO' THE HARVEST HAS BEEN ABUNDANT NOW FOR HUNDREDS OF YEARS AND SCALPING HAS BOWED TO LONG HAIR AND BEARDS. MOST OF US ARE WELL-FED (SOME OF US ARE EVEN OVER-FED.) WE HAVE MUCH MORE THAN THE PILGRIMS HAD TO BE THANKFUL FOR. BUT WHEN WE "give thanks" WE SEEM TO MISS THE WHOLE POINT...

WE SAY "thank you" TO THE CHECKER AT THE SUPERMARKET...

WE SHOW GRATITUDE TO THE BOY WHO HELPS CARRY OUR BUNDLES...

WE GIVE MOM A "THANK-YOU KISS" (XX) BECAUSE SHE IS SUCH A GOOD COOK AND THE TURKEY TASTED DEE-LISH!!

BUT WE HAVE MOSTLY FORGOTTEN THAT WE SHOULD BE GRATEFUL TO GOD... BECAUSE ALL GOOD THINGS COME FROM THE GENEROSITY OF HIS MERCY.

AND THERE WOULD BE NO
TURKEY, NO
DRESSING, NO
CORN-ON-THE-COB, NO
SWEET POTATO,
MINCEMEAT, OR
PUMPKIN PIE, AND
NO ALKA-SELTZER

...WITHOUT GOD'S OFFICIAL O.K.

BUT THERE'S MORE THAN JUST TURKEY TO BE THANKFUL FOR. MORE THAN JUST FRIENDLY INDIANS:

THERE'S OUR SPIRITUAL SCALPS!

GOD IS RESPONSIBLE FOR GIVING US LIFE AND THE ABUNDANT HARVESTS IT BRINGS. WHEN WE WERE ALL FAR FROM HIM, HE DREW NEAR TO US.

IT IS OUR nature NOT TO BE THANKFUL TO GOD... THAT'S CALLED SIN.

BUT GOD HIMSELF PROVIDED A WAY FOR US TO BE CLOSE TO HIM, IN FELLOWSHIP WITH HIM, SO THAT WE MIGHT ENJOY AN ABUNDANT HARVEST IN OUR SOULS

SO THAT WE MIGHT BE SAVED FROM ETERNAL STARVATION AND ENJOY ETERNAL LIFE.

SIT DOWN TO A
THANKSGIVING
DINNER WITH
JESUS, THE ONE
WHO SACRIFICED
HIMSELF SO
THAT WE MIGHT
SPEND ETERNITY

FEASTING ON
THE LOVE
OF GOD

"FOR GOD SO LOVED THE
WORLD THAT HE GAVE
HIS ONLY BEGOTTEN
SON, THAT WHOSOEVER
BELIEVES IN HIM
SHOULD NOT
PERISH BUT
HAVE EVERLASTING LIFE"
JOHN 3:16

Why Do We

Not Know It?

No one people possesses all the wisdom in the world. True, the Passover Haggadah* is complimentary in its assertion that all Jews are wise: Einstein was a mental giant, and so were Herzl, Weizmann, and Ben-Gurion, to mention a few.

For more than nineteen centuries we Jews have been living in a world charged with our ideas, imbued with our idealism, fired by a religion cradled by us. For after all is said and done, was not Jesus a Jew? Were not his first followers Jews? Was not the New Testament written by Jews? Was not Eretz Israel* the soil from which sprang the religion of hundreds of millions of people?

We must admit that there are among non-Jews many who are thinkers, philosophers, poets, writers, painters, scientists, and pure and noble souls to whom Jesus is no fantasy. To them he is the embodiment of the noblest God-virtues, whose life and teaching, devotion to truth and justice, sacrificial death, are so pure that no one among mortals approaches him.

To the masses of our people, however, Jesus is not the Messiah because he came contrary to our expectations. The fantastic figure of the Messiah of Judaism who was to come on a striding white charger, beclouded our vision of the deeper meaning of our Holy Scriptures.

The Prophet Micah, in chapter 5, verse 1, tells that the Messiah was to be born in Bethlehem. The Prophet Isaiah, chapter 53, portrays a suffering Messiah. Psalm 16:10 speaks of his humiliation and triumph over death. All this, and more!

Then why do we Jews not know it? Why do we not recognize Jesus as our Messiah? It is because our Bible is a sealed book to us, and because so-called Christians, in their blindness, have persecuted us until the very visage of our Messiah has become disfigured for us.

Gradually, thinking people are coming to realize that to properly understand Jesus and his message he must be restored into the Jewish framework.

Constantin Brunner, an outstanding Jewish philosopher, makes this comment in the last chapter of his challenging work, "Anti-Semitism and the Jew."

"What is this? Is it only the Jew who is unable to see and hear all that others see and hear? . . . Is Christ to be of no importance to us Jews? Understand, then, what we shall do: we shall bring him back to us. . . . His profound and holy words, and all that is true and heart-appealing in the New Testament must from now on be heard in our synagogues and taught to our children, in order that the wrong we had committed may be made good, and the curse turned into a blessing, and that he at last may find us who has been seeking after us."

If Jesus had been a Greek and all the world except Greece should pay him homage, we would say that Greece was stupid.

Why do we not know it?

"An Eye for An Eye"

In the book of Exodus, chapter 21, verses 23 and 24 we read: "If any harm follows, then you shall give life for life, eye for eye, tooth for tooth, hand for hand, foot for foot . . ."

These are harsh words, and in the New Testament, in the 5th chapter of the Gospel of Matthew, verses 38 to 42, Jesus comments on them by saying: "You have heard that it was said, 'An eye for an eye and a tooth for a tooth.' But I say to you, Do not resist one who is evil. But if any one strikes you on the right cheek, turn to him the other also; and if any one would sue you and take your coat, let him have your cloak as well; and if any one forces you to go one mile, go with him two miles. Give to him who begs from you, and do not refuse him who would borrow from you."

In the world today there still exists the rule "an eye for an eye." As you do to me, so will I do to you. Laws of state and country are based upon this principle. Ethically it is not a lofty principle. It has its basis in the physical nature of man which differs little from that of the beast.

To strike back is a natural reaction. When struck one strikes back; when insulted one retaliates, automatically and in-

13

stinctively, before one has had time to think about it. One does not need to have courage or wisdom to react in this way.

This is the reaction of the animal. This is the weapon of self-defense. This is "an eye for an eye" which enslaves and causes actions to be dependent on another's behavior.

However, one should not be governed by the law of the jungle, but by intellect and reason. One should be free to act after evaluating an action, based on a higher moral standard, and not on a decision made by someone else.

Jesus speaks out against animal behavior. One should not act like an animal but like an intelligent human being. Each such victory of the spirit over "flesh and blood" leaves one a better and a stronger person.

The New Testament Scriptures record a number of admonitions along this line. In the 22nd chapter of Matthew, verses 36 to 40, when Jesus was asked which was the great commandment in the Law, he answered: "You shall love the Lord your God with all your heart, and with all your soul, and with all your mind. This is the first and great commandment. And the second is like it. You shall love your neighbor as yourself."

The story of the good Samaritan, as recorded in the Gospel of Luke, chapter 10, verses 30 to 37, points out that he who shows mercy is a neighbor to one in need.

Saul-Paul, writing to the Romans, chapter 12, verses 17 to 21, says: "Render to no man evil for evil . . . be at peace with all men. Avenge not yourself . . . be not overcome of evil, but overcome evil with good."

The Song of Love, the 13th chapter of I Corinthians, is not only beautiful reading, but strikes at the very heart of human behavior. "Love is patient and kind; love is not jealous or boastful; it is not arrogant or rude . . . ."

One can reach the high level of behavior by repaying good for evil when beastly instincts are conquered and vengeance replaced with love. Only then can one say, "You can act toward me as you choose, you can do me the greatest injustice, but you have no power over me to make me pay you back in your own coin, or force me to descend to your level. You are free to choose your line of conduct — I am free to choose mine. I will not be ruled by you, but by divine truth and justice."

Only in this way can we be free. It isn't easy, but it is the hope of the world.

Israel's

Peculiar

Position

By ERIC HOFFER

The Jews are a peculiar people: things permitted to other nations are forbidden to the Jews.

Other nations drive out thousands, even millions of people and there is no refugee problem. Russia did it; Poland and Czecho-slovakia did it; Turkey drove out a million Greeks; Indonesia threw out heaven knows how many Chinese—and no one says a word about refugees.

But in the case of Israel, the displaced Arabs have become eternal refugees. Everyone insists that Israel must take back every single Arab. Arnold Toynbee calls the displacement of the Arabs an atrocity greater than any committed by the Nazis.

Other nations when victorious on the battlefield dictate peace terms. But when Israel is victorious it must sue for peace. Everyone expects the Jews to be the only real Christians in the world.

Other nations when they are defeated survive and recover. But should Israel be defeated it would be destroyed. Had the Arabs triumphed in the 6-Day War and the Yom Kippur War, they would have wiped Israel off the map, and no one would have lifted a finger to save the Jews.

No commitment to the Jews by any government, including our own, is worth the paper it is written on. There is a cry of outrage all over the world when people died in Vietnam or when two Negroes are executed in Rhodesia. But when Hitler slaughtered the six million Jews, no one remonstrated with him.

The Swedes, who were ready to break off diplomatic relations with America because of what we did in Vietnam, did not let out a peep when Hitler was slaughtering Jews. They sent Hitler choice iron ore, and ball bearings, and serviced his troop trains to Norway.

The Jews are alone in the world. If Israel survives, it will be solely because of Jewish efforts. And Jewish resources.

Yet at this moment Israel is our only reliable and unconditional ally. We can rely more on Israel than Israel can rely on us. And one has only to imagine what would have happened had the Arabs and their Russian backers won the wars to realize how vital the survival of Israel is to America and the West in general.

I have a premonition that will not leave me; as it goes with Israel so will it go with all of us. Should Israel perish the holocaust will be upon us.

Israel must live!

To the Author of

"De Profundis"

By MILDRED ALBERT GREENFIELD

When dawning waits at doors of day
　　That happy wingéd hour,
When evening draws the shades of dusk
　　Asleep each wayside flower;
Amid the turmoil or the hush
　　Of life's incessant roll,
O Israel, the Nazarene
　　Has mercy on thy soul.

His loving heart is touched with grief
   Because of thy despair,
He understands the lonely soul
   That writhes in anguished prayer.
He fain would draw thee to His heart
   And tint thy life with Hope,
His nail-pierced hands are trying now
   To lift thee o'er life's slope.

The loving shepherd wanders o'er
   The meadows and the hills,
His cloak is rent, His feet are worn,
   His heart with yearning fills,
T'is Israel He seeketh now
   His chosen, kindred race,
He'll help thee bear thy burdened cross,
   With love thy heart embrace.

Ah, weary, storm-tossed Israel,
   Look up with joy and peace,
The Master hovers strangely near,
   His vigils never cease,
He does have mercy and forgive,
   With love thy sins atone,
Reach out and clasp His waiting Hand
   And never be alone.

See: RAISINS AND ALMONDS, p. 9.

Walking Alone

By MAX I. REICH

In all the deeper experiences of life the soul must tread a solitary way. There are blessings that come to us through our being component parts of the family, or the community. But those which have to do with our eternal relationship find us in our individuality dealing directly with the realities of the unseen.

There are no greater mysteries than are wrapped up in the two small words: "God" and "I". It will take us all our days, and then the work will have only begun, to find out their depths.

Jacob, we are told, was "left alone. And a man wrestled with him until the break of day." It was the crisis of his life and he had to go through it alone. He bore the marks of that midnight struggle to the end, for he came out of it a crippled and broken, yet divinely blessed man. In the dust he became a prince. In the loneliness he saw God face to face, and the heavenly vision stamped his character with an indelible mark.

Jacob was by no means an amiable character. His brother Esau appeals to the observer much more at first sight. But Jacob was a man whose spirit reached out after the divine. Angels never appeared to the man who preferred the mess of pottage to the privilege of priestly office in the patriarchal succession. Esau never had a Peniel, never cared to be alone with God.

Saul of Tarsus caught a glimpse of the purpose of God for his life when he heard the voice that spoke to him out of the midst of the brightness on the Damascus road. Saul conferred not with flesh and blood, neither did he turn to the older apostles, but retired into Arabia, there to listen to that still small voice of calm that succeeded the earthquake, whirlwind and fire, experiences through which he had passed. And out of that silence, that aloneness and solitude, he came forth the apostle of the nations.

And in this selfsame school of aloneness with God witnesses to divine Truth are still being formed and qualified for service in our busy, fussy, and talkative twentieth century.

Sparks from the Anvil

The order of the universe reveals God as the great Mathematician.

The beauty of the universe reveals Him as the great Poet-Artist.

The harmony of the universe reveals Him as the great Musician.

The Gospel reveals Him as the great Lover, and Jesus the Messiah is His great Love Song.

We must not be afraid to take evidence from our hearts as well as from our heads. The head, in fact, apart from the heart, is a poor thinker.

I can be a lover of flowers without knowing botany;

I can be a lover of the stars without knowing astronomy;

I can be a lover of the Messiah Jesus without knowing theology.

Man is continually choosing the wrong man:
Abraham chose Ishmael; Isaac, Esau; Joseph, Manasseh.
But Ishmael had to be cast out; Esau left out; Manasseh
crossed out.

WHAT DO MEN LIVE BY?

NOT BY BREAD ALONE: You may satisfy a man's physical wants,
but he will still be unhappy.
NOT BY TRUTH ALONE: You may give to a man the benefits of
higher education, and he will still be unsatisfied.
NOT BY BEAUTY ALONE: You may gratify a man's aesthetic
sensibilities, but the need within him remains unmet; he cries
out for more.
NOT BY LOVE ALONE: You may surround a man with friends,
lovers, and affectionate relatives, and yet he will be a seeker
for that which no earthly love can give him.
We live by every word that proceedeth out of the mouth
of the Lord.
We need God—His self-revelation, the vision of His face,
the declaration of His saving truth.
Our spiritual natures cry out for the living God, and the living
God is revealed in His incarnate Son, the Messiah Jesus.

MY EPITAPH

I do not want an epitaph upon my grave.
I know, full well, death levels all—
Wise, fool, king, slave.
But if you really think it well, when I am gone,
To note how I have lived on earth,
Say this alone:
"He fought a losing fight, until this truth he learned:
The life in the Messiah Jesus is God's free gift,
And never earned."

There Are Two
Seas in Israel

By BRUCE BARTON

There are two seas in Israel.

One is fresh, and fish are in it. Splashes of green adorn its banks. Trees spread their branches over it, and stretch out their thirsty roots to sip of its healing water.

Along the shores the children play as children played when the Messiah Jesus was there. He loved it. He could look across its silver surface when he spoke his parables. And on a rolling plain not far away he fed five thousand people.

The river Jordan makes this sea with sparkling water from the hills. So it laughs in the sunshine. And men build their homes near to it, and birds their nests; and every kind of life is happier because it is there.

The river Jordan flows on south into another sea.

Here is no splash of fish, no fluttering leaf, no song of birds, no children's laughter. Travelers choose another route, unless on urgent business. The air hangs heavy above its waters, and neither man, nor beast, nor fowl will drink.

What makes this mighty difference in these neighbor seas?

Not the river Jordan. It empties the same good water into both. Not the soil in which they lie; not the country round about.

This is the difference. The Sea of Galilee receives but does not keep the Jordan. For every drop that flows into it another drop flows out. The giving and receiving go on in equal measure.

The other sea is shrewder, hoarding its income jealously.

It will not be tempted into any generous impulse. Every drop it gets it keeps.

The Sea of Galilee gives and lives. This other sea gives nothing. It is named the Dead Sea.

There are two kinds of people in the world.

There are two seas in Israel.

Courtesy of L. K. Helldorfer

The Psalm-Song Book

The book of Psalms, the first and most popular book of the Writings, the Ketuvim, occupies an important place in Holy Scriptures.

Among the one hundred and fifty psalms are three which have only three verses: Psalms 131, 133, and 134. Psalm 117 has only two verses, while Psalm 119 has 176 verses.

Many psalms are hymns of praise and gratitude, expressing thankfulness for help extended and refuge found in time of danger and distress. These glorify God, his power, and his loving-kindness as manifested in nature or shown to Israel. This group embraces about one-third of the Psalter.

There are psalms dealing with supplication, the burden of which is fervent prayer for the improving of conditions, the restoration of Israel to grace, and the repentance of sinners. These are inspired by consciousness of guilt, and not by a sense of unmerited affliction. Their key-note is open confession of sin and transgression prompted by ardent repentance and the yearning for forgiveness.

Included are psalms which speak of righteous conduct and speech, and caution against improper behavior and attitude. They exhibit a high degree of perfection of language and a wealth of metaphor, as well as rhythm of thought. Several are acrostic or alphabetic in arrangement, the letter of the Hebrew alphabet occurring in various positions.

The Book of Psalms is said to have been the hymnbook during the existence of the Second Temple, and by tradition David is regarded as the writer of most of it. Whether David composed and/or compiled it is not the most important thing. The ascription of authorship to him is due in part to the tendency to credit the chief literary production of the nation to a dominating personality.

According to Talmudic tradition psalms were sung by the Levites; some think that they were sung by the people, perhaps chanted antiphonally. We do know that the Book of Psalms is without doubt the best known portion of the Bible, not only among Jews, because it has become an integral part of our liturgy, but also among non-Jews who have incorporated many of the psalms into their worship service as hymns.

Psalm 43 consists of five verses and is a strong assurance of faith and hope in God. The psalmist begins with: "Judge me, O God, and plead my cause . . ."

מִשְפָּט מִיך, אָ גאָט, מיין רעטער

1 מִשְפָּט מִיך, אָ גאָט, מיין רעטער,
מיט מיין שׂונא קריג מיין קריג;
הער מיין שטילע, טיפע תפילה,
וואָס איך בעט צו דיר און שיק.

2 ביסט מיין אָנלען, ביסט מיין שטאַרקייט, –
וואָס בין איך פאַרלאָזט פון דיר?
כ'גיי אום הילפלאָ און פאַרעלנט,
ווען דער שׂונא דריקט אויף מיר.

3 זאָל דיין ליכט און זאָל דיין אֱמֶת
מיך באַגלייטן דורך דער וועלט,
ביז איך וועל דיין באַרג באַשטייגן
צו דעם הייליקן געצעלט.

4 כ'וועל פאַר דיין מִזבֵּחַ קניען,
גאָט, מיין גאָט, מיין גרויסע פרייד!
כ'וועל מיט האַרף און ליד דיר דינען,
לויבן דיך אין אייביקייט!

כאָר: זאָג, וואָס בייגסטו זיך נשָׁמָה?
זאָג, וואָס ברענגט דיר ווי און צער?
האָף צו גאָט, ער וועט דיר העלפן, –
כ'וועל נאָך לויבן גאָט מיין האר.

Judge Me, God of My Salvation

PSALM 43

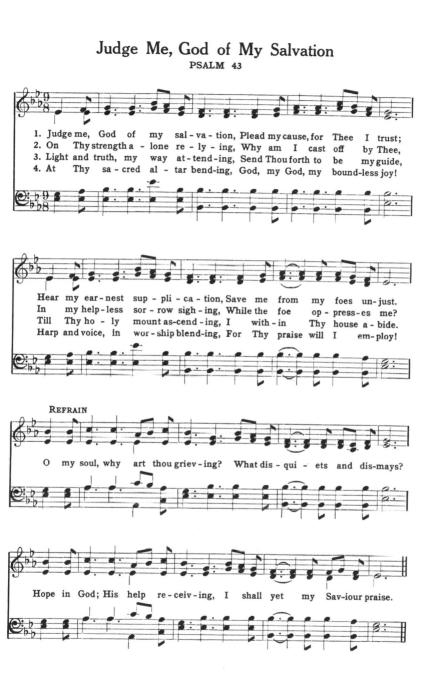

1. Judge me, God of my sal - va - tion, Plead my cause, for Thee I trust;
2. On Thy strength a - lone re - ly - ing, Why am I cast off by Thee,
3. Light and truth, my way at - tend - ing, Send Thou forth to be my guide,
4. At Thy sa - cred al - tar bend - ing, God, my God, my bound-less joy!

Hear my ear - nest sup - pli - ca - tion, Save me from my foes un - just.
In my help - less sor - row sigh - ing, While the foe op - press - es me?
Till Thy ho - ly mount as - cend - ing, I with - in Thy house a - bide.
Harp and voice, in wor - ship blend - ing, For Thy praise will I em - ploy!

REFRAIN

O my soul, why art thou griev - ing? What dis - qui - ets and dis - mays?

Hope in God; His help re - ceiv - ing, I shall yet my Sav - iour praise.

Psalm 51 is a reflection of King David's repentance when he asked for a pure heart. It was most likely written after the Prophet Nathan came to him when he sinned with Bathsheba. Listen to the cry of the sinner: "Have mercy upon me, O God . . ."

גאָט זיי לייטזעליק צו מיר

תהלים נ"א

1 גאָט, זיי לײַטזעליק צו מיר,
איך פאַרלאָז מיך נאָר אויף דיר;
דײַן דערבאַרעמונג איז גרויס,
מעק מיר די עבירות אויס;
מאָך מיך קלאָר און מאָך מיך רײן,
וואַש פון זינד מיך מײַן און מײַן.

2 איך בין זינדיק, איך בין שלעכט,
דו באַגערסט נאָר וואָר און רעכט.
ביסט מײַן גואֵל, דו אַלײן,
גיב דײַן חכמה מיר פאַרשטײן,
הער מײַן תפילה, מײַן געשרײַ:
וואַש מיך ווײסער פון דעם שניי.

3 גאָט פון גנאָד, מײַן האַרץ באַנײַ,
כ'וועל דיר דינען וואָר און טרײַ.
וואַרף מיך נישט אַוועק פון דיר,
גיב דײַן גײַסט אַרײַן אין מיר.
לײַז מיך אויס פון שולד און לײד,
שטאַרק דאָס האַרץ מיר מיט דײַן פרײַד.

4 איך וועל לערנען, האַר, דײַן וועג
דעם, וואָס איז אין זינד אַוועק.
האַר, מעק אָפ מיר מײַנע זינד,
כ'וועל דיך לויבן ווי אַ קינד;
מײַנע ליפן נאָר באַריר —
וועט מײַן מויל לויב זינגען דיר.

God, Be Merciful to Me

PSALM 51

1. God, be mer - ci - ful to me, On Thy grace I rest my plea;
2. I am e - vil, born in sin; Thou de - sir - est truth with - in.
3. Gra - cious God, my heart re - new, Make my spir - it right and true;
4. Sin - ners then shall learn from me And re - turn, O God, to Thee;

Plen - teous in com - pas - sion Thou, Blot out my trans-gres-sions now;
Thou a - lone my Sav - iour art, Teach Thy wis - dom to my heart;
Cast me not a - way from Thee, Let Thy Spir - it dwell in me;
Sav - iour, all my guilt re - move, And my tongue shall sing Thy love;

Wash me, make me pure with - in, Cleanse, O cleanse me from my sin,
Make me pure, Thy grace be - stow, Wash me whit - er than the snow,
Thy sal - va - tion's joy im - part, Stead - fast make my will - ing heart,
Touch my si - lent lips, O Lord, And my mouth shall praise ac - cord,

Wash me, make me pure with - in, Cleanse, O cleanse me from my sin.
Make me pure, Thy grace be - stow, Wash me whit - er than the snow.
Thy sal - va - tion's joy im - part, Stead - fast make my will - ing heart.
Touch my si - lent lips, O Lord, And my mouth shall praise ac - cord.

Perhaps one of the best known psalms is the 23rd, known as the Shepherd's Song, beginning with the words: "The Lord is my shepherd; I shall not want."

גאָט איז מיין גוטער פּאַסטוך

תהלים כ"ג

1 גאָט איז מיין גוטער פּאַסטוך,
ער פירט מיך און באַהיט,
מיט גוטסקייט ער באַלאַסט מיך, —
סע פעלט מיר גאָרנישט ניט.
אויף גרינע לאָנקעס מאַכט ער
מיך רוען אומגעשטערט,
ביי שטילע טייכן פירט ער
אַרום מיך מיט זיין הערט.

2 צוליב זיין נאָמענסוועגן
באַפרייט ער מיך פון לייד;
ער פירט מיך אויף די שטעגן
פון זיין גערעכטיקייט.
דיין רוט, דיין אָנלען טרייסט מיך,
וואָס שרעקט מיך דען די נויט,
אַז דו אַליין באַגלייטסט מיך
אויך דורך דעם טאָל פון טויט?!

3 מיין שפּייז טוסטו מיר ווייַלן
צו לְהַכעיס מיינע פיינט;
זאַלבסט מיך מיט דיינע אייַלן,
דיין טרונק אין בעכער שיינט.
גאָט, פירן דורך דעם לעבן
דיין גוטסקייט זאָל מיך בלויז;
אַ היים וועסטו מיר געבן
אויף אייביק אין דיין הויז.

The Lord My Shepherd Holds Me

PSALM 23

1. The Lord my Shep-herd holds me With-in His ten-der care,
2. What-ev-er ill be-tides me, He will re-store and bless;
3. My food Thou dost ap-point me, Sup-plied be-fore my foes;

And with His flock He folds me, No want shall find me there.
For His Name's sake He guides me In paths of right-eous-ness.
With oil Thou dost a-noint me, My cup of bliss o'er-flows.

In pas-tures green He feeds me, With plen-ty I am blest;
Thy rod and staff shall cheer me In death's dark vale and shade,
Thy good-ness, Lord, shall guide me, Thy mer-cy cheer my way;

By qui-et streams He leads me And makes me safe-ly rest.
For Thou wilt then be near me: I shall not be a-fraid.
A home Thou wilt pro-vide me With-in Thy house for aye.

In the New Testament, in the twenty-sixth chapter of the Gospel According to Matthew, verse thirty, we read that after Jesus celebrated the Passover with his disciples they sang a hymn. What did they sing? According to tradition they sang the Hallel, Psalms 113 to 118, beginning with the words: "O give thanks unto the Lord; for He is good."

The music of the world has been enriched because of the contribution by us Jews. Through us the world received the Torah,* through us came the prophets, and through us came the Messiah Jesus, the world's Saviour. The Christian Church sings our songs, reads our Scriptures, prays to our God, and has hope in the world to come.

Let us sing a new song, the song of the Lamb (Revelation 15:5).

My Daughter and the Sphinx

By MOISHE ROSEN

Near Central Park in New York City there stands a great museum called the American Museum of Natural History. It is known the world over for its priceless collections of fossils, mammals, reptiles, gems, extinct animals, archaeological curiosities, specimens from every field in the realm of earth science.

On a Sunday afternoon, like many another parent, I took my little girl for a tour of the museum. Together we strolled down softly lighted corridors, gazed in wonder at trays of rare jewels, savored the mystery of life in the South American rain forest, gaped at the huge whale that hangs suspended from the ceiling of one hall.

She was just four years old. She clutched my hand and moved closer when she saw the skeleton of the dinosaur that takes up the entire length of one large room, and she squealed delightedly at the displays of wild animals, mounted in family groups in simulated natural habitat.

My hobby is photography. Like any fond parent I had my camera ready. I have many a slide that I took that Sunday afternoon, and I have one that I value highly. It is no prize-winning snapshot. I couldn't exhibit it or sell it for publication. But I cherish it because it has special meaning for me. It was taken in the Egyptian room.

My little girl was far too young to appreciate the art and science of ancient Egypt, but she was delighted with the color and pageantry, the paintings of birds and animals, the statues of animals, and of animals that look like people.

In my snapshot she is standing before a stone Sphinx. The Sphinx weighs more than a ton, and it is mounted on a pedestal higher than my daughter is tall. She must stand back and gaze up to get a good look at it. There she stands, captured by my camera, with her curls down over her shoulders in the fashion of twentieth-century children, wearing a coat we got her at Macy's, ankleted feet thrust into her flat-heeled little girl's shoes, planted solidly on firm ground. To me this is a wonder, this daughter of the year 5729 stopping to marvel at an image that was fashioned thirty-five centuries before she was born.

You see, my child is Jewish. Her mother's forebears came from Germany two generations ago. Mine came from Russia about the same time. Beyond that there is a gap and we know nothing of our antecedents. But my child's distant ancestors were slaves in Egypt. They endured hard servitude under cruel taskmasters. They may have labored to produce the very image at which she stopped to gaze.

My child stands there, free-born, lively, with many years before her. But her ancestors' taskmasters, where are they? Their proud kingdom was leveled, their people themselves became slaves, their wisdom was lost, and their treasures were sacked to become museum curiosities. Their idols were thrown down and crushed, their religion disappeared into antiquity. Their monuments are now tourist attractions.

But we, my daughter's people, we are here. Our synagogues grace the avenues of all great cities. Our writers have their books in every library. Our scientists have unlocked secrets that even the Egyptians did not know. Our physicians have blessed and healed multitudes. Our men have occupied high government office. After two thousand years of eclipse, our nation has been born anew and stands among the other nations.

But why have we survived? The Egyptians were not our only oppressors. They were only the first of a long line. The Assyrians and Babylonians in turn made us captive. The Romans showed us no mercy. The horrors of recent years have surpassed anything the Egyptians dreamed of. But where are these empires? Their relics, too, have found a place in the world's museums. We remain, my daughter and I and our kinsmen.

Why have we survived? It would be human to say that it was because we are a proud, independent people who rebelled at being slaves, too virile and hardy ever to be extinguished, too exclusive to merge with our neighbors and lose identity.

Yes, it would be human to say so. But it would not be true. When we search our own sacred texts for some key, some clue, some hidden strength, something of merit, we find that our own prophets scold us, and even Moses accuses us.

Was it because of our pride, our love of freedom? No, my people, the historical record says no. Don't you remember the story of the Exodus from Egypt, how in the face of every difficulty our forebears wept and wanted to return to Egypt?

"Is not this the word that we spoke unto thee in Egypt, saying: Let us alone, that we may serve the Egyptians? For it were better for us to serve the Egyptians, than that we should die in the wilderness." (Exodus 14:12)

Was it because we were of such great numbers that it would be impossible to exterminate us? No, for the Scripture says:

"And the Lord shall scatter you among the peoples, and ye shall be left few in number among the nations, whither the Lord shall lead you away." (Deuteronomy 4:27)

Was it because we were too exclusive to merge with our neighbors and lose our identity? No, for the record says:

"In those days also saw I the Jews that had married women of Ashdod, of Ammon, and of Moab; and their children spoke half in the speech of Ashdod, and could not speak in the Jews' language." (Nehemiah 13:23, 24)

Was it because we were a virile hardy people? No, for the prophet Isaiah says:

"On what part will ye yet be stricken, seeing ye stray away more and more? The whole head is sick, and the whole heart faint. From the sole of the foot even unto the head there is no soundness in it; but wounds, and bruises, and festering sores." (Isaiah 1:5, 6)

Was it because of our righteousness? No, for the Scripture says:

"Ah sinful nation, a people laden with iniquity, a seed of evil-doers, children that deal corruptly; they have forsaken the Lord, they have despised the Holy One of Israel, they are turned away backward." (Isaiah 1:4)

Or was it our faithfulness? No, for Moses himself says:

"Of the Rock that begot thee thou wast unmindful, and didst forget God that bore thee." (Deuteronomy 32:18)

Yet we are here. And I thought of something else, in the museum, watching my daughter. We were the conquerors, my child and I. We have survived, our oppressors have vanished. We must come to museums to study their way of life. They are not here to look at us.

Yes, our own prophets scold us. But they comfort us meanwhile. And Moses accuses us. But Moses blesses us also. A deeper search of our own sacred texts will show why we have survived, whose hand it is that preserved us, whose purposes are being carried out.

The Psalmist tells us, "Behold, He that keepeth Israel shall neither slumber nor sleep." (Psalm 121:4) And He has not slept, not during the bondage in Egypt, nor during the successive oppressions of Assyria, Babylon and Rome, nor in the more recent oppressions of Germany and Russia. Through it all He was keeping us. That is why we have survived and our oppressors have perished.

We have survived because God made a promise. He made a promise to our father Abraham, of a land, a nation, and a blessing.

"Now the Lord said unto Abram: 'Get thee out of thy country, and from thy kindred, and from thy father's house, unto the land that I will show thee. And I will make of thee a great nation, and I will bless thee, and make thy name great; and be thou a blessing. And I will bless them that bless thee, and him that curseth thee will I curse; and in thee shall all the families of the earth be blessed." (Genesis 12:1-3)

The land was Palestine, the nation was Israel, the blessing was the Messiah.

"And it shall come to pass in that day, that the root of Jesse, that standeth for an ensign of the peoples, unto him shall the nations seek." (Isaiah 11:10)

We have survived because God has a purpose. His purpose was to bless all the people of the world through us.

"God be gracious unto us, and bless us; may He cause His face to shine toward us; Selah. That Thy way may be known upon earth, Thy salvation among all nations. Let the peoples give thanks unto Thee, O God; let the peoples give thanks unto Thee, all of them. O let the nations be glad and sing for joy; for Thou wilt judge the peoples with equity, and lead the nations upon earth. Selah. Let the peoples give thanks unto Thee, O God; let the peoples give thanks unto Thee, all of them. The earth hath yielded her increase; may God, our own God, bless us. May God bless us; and let all the ends of the earth fear Him." (Psalm 67)

"They are Israelites, and to them belong the sonship, the glory, the covenants, the giving of the law, the worship, and the promises; to them belong the patriarchs, and of their race, according to the flesh, is the Christ (Messiah). God who is over all be blessed for ever. Amen." (Romans 9: 4, 5)

We have survived because God has a destiny for us. Our sufferings have had a goal. God called us once that through us He might transmit His revelation to the whole world. He called us again that through us His Messiah might come to bless the whole world. He is calling us again that through us He might be glorified before the whole world.

"Arise, shine, for thy light is come, and the glory of the Lord is risen upon thee. For, behold, darkness shall cover the earth, and gross darkness the peoples; but upon thee the Lord will arise, and His glory shall be seen upon thee. And nations shall walk at thy light, and kings at the brightness of thy rising." (Isaiah 60:1-3)

THE GOSPELS

AND RABBINIC

LITERATURE

Every word that Shakespeare ever wrote, or Lincoln ever uttered, is in the dictionary, and yet, in spite of dictionaries and lexicons, there was but one Shakespeare and but one Lincoln.

There have been many attemps to prove the unprovable, and Graetz, Geiger, and others, have gone to great lengths to point out unsuccessfully that the pithy sayings of Jesus in the Gospels have their origin in Rabbinic literature.

If the Gospels were a plagiarization of Rabbinic literature, then the question that would suggest itself is: Why have not the sayings of the Rabbis and their ethical precepts shown such virility, won such universal approbation, and become the Torah* of the intelligent man as have the Gospels?

Whose sayings have held greater sway, or are better known—those of Rabbis Shammai and Chanina Ben Dosa, or those of Rabbi Yeshua-Jesus? The fallacy of critics of the Gospels lies in an utter disregard of what is commonly called the critical apparatus. When, for example, the Talmud, in Sanhedrin 100a, attributes to Rabbi Meir a saying identical in spirit, as well as in phraseology, with that uttered by Jesus in Matthew 7:2, it should be noted as a matter of historic accuracy that Rabbi Meir was not even born when Jesus spoke those words.

That there exist parallels between the Talmud and the Gospels is undeniable, but a close study reveals what Rabbi Emil Hirsch once declared, that in the Gospels the sayings carry the stamp of personality which constitutes their originality.

Claude G. Montefiore, Liberal Jewish leader and scholar, has this to say in his commentary on the Gospels (The Synoptic Gospels, Vol. 1, p. 103):

"A great book is more than its own sentences taken singly or disjointedly. A great personality is more than the record of its teachings, and the teaching is more than the bits of it taken one by one. It must be viewed as a whole. It must be judged as a whole. It has a spirit, an aroma, which evaporates when its elements or fragments are looked at separately. This piecemeal way of looking at a book, a teaching, a person, is perhaps partially one of the evil results of Jewish legalism.

"There is a certain spirit and glow about the teaching of Jesus which you either appreciate or fail to appreciate. You cannot recognize or do justice to it by saying: 'The teaching of Jesus comprises the following maxims and injunctions. Of these some are borrowed from the Old Testament, some are parallelled by the Talmud, and a few are impracticable.' The teaching of Jesus, which has had such gigantic effects upon the world, is more and other than a dissected list of injunctions. It is not merely the sum of its parts, it is a whole, a spirit.

"That spirit has characteristics of genius. It is great, stimulating, heroic; it may not always be 'practical' but it is always, or nearly always, big and grand. Even if you find in the Talmud separate or close parallels for 970 out of say 1,000 verses in the Gospels in which Jesus is the speaker, and even if you put them together and make a nice little book of them, you would not have produced a substitute of equal religious value. The unity, the aroma, the spirit, the genius, would all have fled. Or rather, you could not infuse them into your elegant collection of fragments and titbits."

Professor Hermann L. Strack, in his monumental commentary on the New Testament in the light of Talmud and Midrash, has brought together several hundred such parallels, showing that in almost every instance where parallels do exist, the authors to whom the Talmud attributes these sayings lived at least one, and in several instances, even three hundred years later than did Jesus.

To attribute the teaching of Jesus to the Talmudic literature is to betray an ignorance of sources and historic data. —See "RAISINS AND ALMONDS," pp. 60-63.

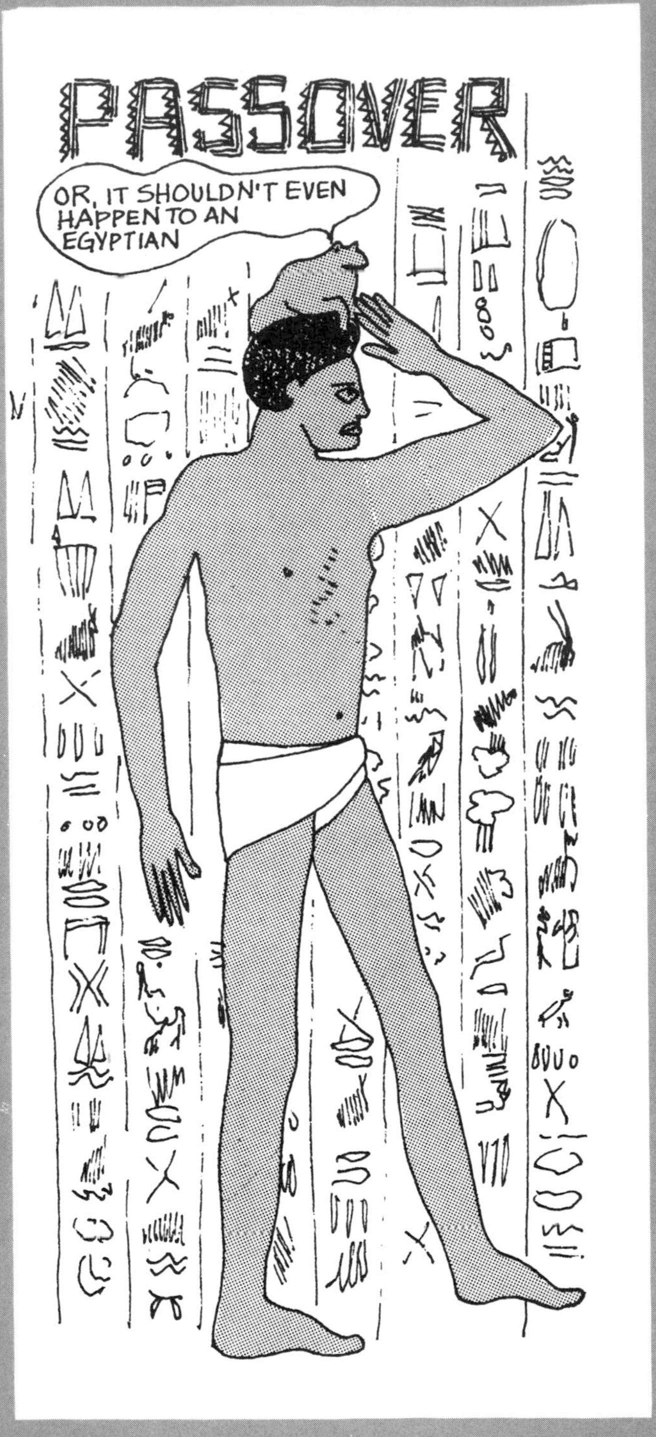
PASSOVER
OR, IT SHOULDN'T EVEN HAPPEN TO AN EGYPTIAN

PHARAOH SAID, "I DON'T KNOW YOU, BUT SINCE YOU ARE LIVING IN MY LAND, YOU CAN BE MY SLAVES. MAKE BRICKS FOR ME AND I'LL LET SOME OF YOU LIVE."

Now, Pharaoh didn't even know the Jews. But more important, he didn't know that the Jews were God's Chosen People. He thought he could do what he wanted and he did...for a long, long time. However, the cry of the Israelites came up before GOD, so GOD sent Moses to say **LET MY PEOPLE GO!**

OY VEY! OY VEY! OY VEY!

Pharaoh thought that it was rather insolent, disrespectful and otherwise obnoxious for Moses to behave this way; and Pharaoh said "NO! NO! TEN TIMES NO!" ~~卌~~ ~~卌~~

(He should have had the good sense to say YES from the beginning)

AS IT WAS, all the Egyptians got boils on their bodies, frogs in their soup, darkness over their land, and all kinds of other **tsuris*** just because Pharaoh said **NO** to GOD

NO
NO
NO
NO
NO
NO
NO
NO!

IN THE END THINGS GOT SO HEAVY, PHARAOH FINALLY HAD TO SAY YES...THOUGH HE STILL REALLY DIDN'T WANT TO.

You would think that some nations would learn a lesson from history, but they don't. They still say NO! NO! with regard to the Jews; and what's worse, they don't even know that they are saying NO to GOD.

* troubles, woes, misery, sufferings

The HAMANS, HERODS & HITLERS of the world still think they can foil the plans of the **ALMIGHTY**

you see GOD CREATED THE JEWISH PEOPLE TO BLESS THE NATIONS.* IT WAS THROUGH THE JEWISH PEOPLE THAT THE BIBLE CAME INTO BEING. IT WAS THROUGH THE JEWISH PEOPLE THAT GOD DEMONSTRATED HIS FAITHFULNESS. IT WAS THROUGH THE **JEWISH** PEOPLE THAT THE **MESSIAH JESUS** CAME TO EARTH TO SAVE EVERYONE FROM SIN AND DEATH.

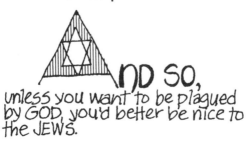

AND SO, unless you want to be plagued by GOD, you'd better be nice to the JEWS.

*GENESIS 12:3 **JOHN 3:16,17

And while you are at it, don't forget one very special JEW named JESUS. HE was the only perfect JEW that ever lived. He died to save all of mankind. And He wants to give us all plague-free lives.

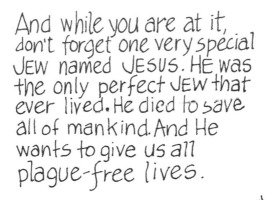

CROAK!

P.S. JEWS: BE NICE TO YOURSELVES. DON'T THINK THAT YOU CAN FOIL GOD'S PLANS EITHER. ACCEPT JESUS AS <u>YOUR</u> MESSIAH. DON'T SAY NO! NO! TO GOD. YOU, MOST OF ALL, SHOULD KNOW — IT DOESN'T WORK

DAYENU*

* ꝺnuf said.

Jesus and Alexander

Jesus and Alexander died at thirty-three,
One lived and died for self; one died for you and me.
The Greek died on a throne; the Jew died on a cross;
One's life a triumph seemed; the other but a loss.
One led vast armies forth; the other walked alone;
One shed a whole world's blood; the other gave his own.
One won the world in life and lost it all in death;
The other lost his life to win the whole world's faith.

Jesus and Alexander died at thirty-three.
One died in Babylon; and one on Calvary.
One gained all for self; and one himself he gave,
One conquered every throne; the other every grave.
The one made himself God; the God made himself less;
The one lived but to blast; the other but to bless.
When died the Greek, forever, fell his throne of swords;
But Jesus died to live forever Lord of Lords.

Jesus and Alexander died at thirty-three,
The Greek made all men slaves; the Jew made all men free.
One built a throne on blood; the other built on love,
The one was born of earth; the other from above;
One won all this earth, to lose all earth and heaven;
The other gave up all, that all to him be given.
The Greek forever died; the Jew forever lives.
He loses all who gets, and wins all things who gives.

Charles Ross Weede

The Most Famous

Town in the World

The most famous town in all the world today is not a turret-crowned metropolis whose canyoned aisles of commerce are thronged with harried multitudes. The most famous town in all the world today is not numbered among the many great ports of entry where the ships of a hundred flags gather from off the seven seas laden with precious cargoes and peopled with men of every tongue and walk of life.

The most famous town in all the world today has no chamber of commerce worth mentioning, no hotel noted for cuisine or accommodations, no mart designed to draw its trade from the far corners of the earth. And yet, four miles from a railroad, and forty from the sea, without appeal to seekers after health or wealth or honor, it stands today closest to the heart of the world of all the towns that are.

The most famous town in all the world today is what it is because two Jews were born there. One of these was a shepherd lad when the call of life's business came to him. With a harp of gold and a heart that knew no fear David stepped out to become a king among his fellows.

The boldness of his deeds and the splendid loveliness of his spirit came down to us in stately words from ancient days. With the passing of the years the sweet singer of Israel passed also, and was gathered to his fathers, leaving to his people a heritage of high hope which has cheered through all times all races of man.

In the fulness of the centuries another Jewish lad first saw the light of earthly day at the natal city of the shepherd boy who became a king. Grown to manhood's estate as a carpenter, traveling from place to place, without home, without office or place, followed of the lowly and pursued by the mighty, besieged by the curious and spurned by the critical, hailed by the ignorant and ridiculed by the wise of his day, done to death at last on a felon's cross, this commoner of Compassion so revealed the soul of God to the soul of man that the aspirations of human kind are twined about the things that he did, and the words that he spoke in those three short years of his recorded ministry.

Small wonder then, that the stable manger that Jesus was born in is the symbol of blessedness of childhood, and the cross of shame whereon he died is now the badge of honor for which brave men have gladly paid all, or that Bethlehem, the little city of David and of the carpenter Prince of Peace, is the most famous town in all the world today—Author Unknown.

The Penitent

By LEO TOLSTOY

There was once a man who lived for seventy years, and lived in sin all that time. He fell ill, but even then did not repent. Only at the last moment, as he was dying, he wept and said:

"Lord, forgive me as you forgave the thief upon the cross."

And as he said these words, his soul left his body. And the soul of the sinner, feeling love towards God and faith in His mercy, went to the gates of heaven, and knocked, asking to be let into the heavenly kingdom.

Then a voice spoke from within the gates:

"What man is it that knocks at the gates of Paradise, and what deeds did he do during his life?"

And the voice of the Accuser replied, recounting all the man's evil deeds, and not a single good one.

Then the voice from within the gates answered:

"Sinners cannot enter the kingdom of heaven. Go away!"

The man said:

"Sir, I hear your voice, but cannot see your face, nor do I know your name."

The voice answered:

"I am Simon Peter, the Apostle."

And the sinner replied:

Have pity on me, Simon Peter. Remember man's weakness and God's mercy. Were you not a disciple of Jesus the

Messiah? Did you not hear his teaching from his own lips, and did you not have his example before you? Remember then how, when he sorrowed and was grieved in spirit, and three times asked you to keep awake and pray, that you slept because your eyes were heavy. And three times he found you sleeping. So it was with me. Remember, also, how you promised to be faithful to death, and yet three times you denied him when he was taken before Caiphas. So it was with me. And remember, too, how when the cock crowed that you went out and wept bitterly. So it was with me. You cannot refuse to let me in."

And the voice behind the gates was silent.

Then the sinner stood a little while, and again began to knock, and to ask to be let into the kingdom of heaven.

And he heard another voice behind the gates, which said:

"Who is this man, and how did he live on earth?"

And the voice of the Accuser again repeated all the sinner's evil deeds, and not a single good one.

And the voice from behind the gates replied:

"Go away! Such sinners cannot live with us in Paradise."

Then the sinner said:

"Sir, I hear your voice, but I cannot see you, nor do I know your name."

And the voice answered:

"I am King David."

The sinner did not despair, nor did he leave the gates of Paradise, but said:

"Have pity on me, King David! Remember man's weakness and God's mercy. God loved you and exalted you among men. You had all: a kingdom, and honor, and riches, and wives, and children; but you saw from your house-top the wife of a poor man, and sin entered into you, and you took the wife of Uriah, and you slew him with the sword of the Ammonites. You, a rich man, took from the poor man his one ewe lamb and killed him. I have done likewise. Remember, then, how you repented, and how you said, 'I acknowledge my transgressions: my sin is ever before me.' I have done the same. You cannot refuse to let me in."

And the voice from within the gates was silent.

The sinner having stood a little while, began knocking again, and asked to be let into the kingdom of heaven. And a third voice was heard within the gates, saying:

"Who is this man, and how has he spent his life on earth?"

And the voice of the Accuser replied for the third time, recounting the sinner's evil deeds, and not mentioning one good deed.

And the voice within the gates said:

"Depart! Sinners cannot enter into the kingdom of heaven."

And the sinner said:

"Your voice I hear, but your face I do not see, neither do I know your name."

Then the voice replied:

"I am John, the beloved disciple of Jesus."

And the sinner rejoiced and said:

"Now surely I shall be allowed to enter. Simon Peter should have let me in because he knows God's mercy; King David should have let me in because he knows man's weakness; and you, John must let me in because you loved much. Was it not you who wrote that God is Love, and that he who loves not, knows not God? And in your old age did you not say to men: 'Brethren, love one another'? How, then, could you look on me with hatred and drive me away? Either you must renounce what you have said, or, loving me, must let me enter into the kingdom of heaven."

Suddenly throughout the heavenly realm there was heard the voice of Jesus saying:

"I came not to call the righteous, but sinners."

Immediately the gates of Paradise opened, and John embraced the penitent sinner and took him into the kingdom of heaven."

AT JERUSALEM

I stood by the Holy City
  Without the Damascus Gate,
While the wind blew soft from the distant sea,
  And the day was wearing late;
And swept its wide horizon
  With reverent lingering gaze
From the rolling uplands of the West
  That slope a hundred ways,
To Olivet's gray terraces
  By Kedron's bed that rise,
Upon whose crest the Crucified
  Was lost to mortal eyes.
And, far beyond to the tawny line
  Where the sun seemed still to fall—
So bright the hue against the blue,
  Of Moab's mountain wall;
And north to the hills of Benjamin,
  Whose springs are flowing yet,
Ramah, and sacred Mizpah,
  Its dome above them set;
And the beautiful words of the Psalmist
  Had meaning before unknown;
As the mountains are round Jerusalem
  The Lord is round His own.

EDNA DEAN PROCTOR

Rome

and Judea

By BENJAMIN DISRAELI

In all church discussions we are apt to forget that the second Testament is avowedly only a supplement. The Messiah Jesus came to complete the Law and the Prophets. Christianity is completed Judaism, or it is nothing. Christianity is incomprehensible without Judaism, as Judaism is incomplete without Christianity.

The Law was not thundered forth from the Capitolian mount; the divine atonement was not fulfilled upon Mons Sacer. No; the order of our priesthood comes directly from Jehovah; and the forms and ceremonies of His church are the regulations of His supreme intelligence.

When Omnipotence deigned to be incarnate, the Ineffable Word did not select a Roman, but a Jewish frame. The prophets were not Romans, but Jews; the apostles were not Romans, but Jews; she who was blessed above all women,

I never heard she was a Roman maiden. No, I should look to a land more distant than Italy, to a city more sacred even than Rome.

The first preachers of the gospel were Jews, and none else; the historians of the gospel were Jews, and none else. For nearly a century no one believed in the good tidings except Jews. They nursed the sacred flame of which they were the consecrated and hereditary depositaries.

And when the time was ripe to diffuse the truth among the nations, it was not a senator of Rome or a philosopher of Athens who was personally appointed by our Lord for that office, but a Jew of Tarsus, who founded the seven churches of Asia.

And that great church, great even amid its terrible corruptions, that has avenged the victory of Titus by subjugating the capital of the Caesars, and has changed every one of the Olympian temples into altars of the God of Sinai and of Calvary, was founded by another Jew, a Jew of Galilee.

From: "Sybil or The Two Nations"

Benjamin Disraeli

Jacob's Ladder

By FRED G. KENDAL

I want to take you with me for a glimpse of the life of a prominent character in Bible history whose experience is a vivid picture of the world in motion today.

In the twenty-eighth chapter of Genesis Jacob is seen fleeing from his father's house, seeking a new home and protection in the house of his uncle Laban. Behind him were the memories of a happy home atmosphere, torn to shreds by his conniving. Following him was the dread of an outraged brother's vengeance, and within him the voice of an accusing conscience.

Jacob sought peace. He thought he could find it by changing his circumstances. He hoped that a different environment would end the strife that had marred his happiness.

Jacob did not realize that he was carrying his burden with him, that the fire from which he fled smoldered in his own breast. The strife which he feared kept company with him wherever he went. He found strife in Laban's house, even as in his father's house

Is it not true that the world, like Jacob, seeks to flee from its house of sorrow; like the ostrich, men would plunge their heads in the sand of activity, and ignore the cyclone that besets their souls! So many think that a change in their circumstances will bring happiness to their hearts. More money, more clothes, better houses, greater luxuries; but when they come they do not decrease the pain, they aggravate it. They bring greater desires to taunt the human breast.

There was an impelling force back of Jacob's fevered journey, it was the voice of God calling him from his selfish ways. The record in the twenty-eighth chapter of Genesis tells us that Jacob lighted upon a certain place. The Hebrew word translated "certain place" is Makom, which means "the presence of God." Jacob lay his wearied head upon a stone and slept. He dreamed and, "Behold, a ladder set up on the earth and the top of it reached to heaven; and, behold, the angels of God ascending and descending on it."

Jacob thought he could run away from God, but he was mistaken. The arms that encircled fear-haunted Jacob were not arms of hate: they were arms of mercy.

How many, like him, think they can run away from God. Some would like to still the voice of conscience by religious exercises, but only find it to be true as David did, who said, "Whither shall I go from thy Spirit, or whither shall I flee from thy presence? If I ascend to heaven, thou art there! If I make my bed in Sheol, thou art there!" You must face God.

A ladder suggests a distance to be overcome, a chasm to be spanned, an obstacle to be surmounted. God was saying to Jacob through the ladder, "You cannot shake yourself and think that you can throw off your misdeeds. There is a distance between you and Me. You are not far away in miles, you are far away in sin. Your sins have separated between you and your God."

Like the leper of old you must cry out in the presence of God, "Unclean! Unclean!" King David exclaimed, "If thou, oh Lord, shouldest regard iniquity, who can stand?"

The presence of a ladder suggests the recognition of an obstacle. In the world today we find many ladders indicating the recognition by people generally that there is something wrong. The many religions that we find in the world are ladders. Buddhist shrines, Mohammedan prayers, cults and isms, all speak of the effort of man to bridge the gulf between himself and his Maker.

A true ladder does not only recognize a problem, it solves it. God was promising Jacob a ladder of mercy through which he could come to the rescue of his run-away servant.

The ladder must touch earth and also touch heaven. A ladder unites separated parties. The hope of Jacob and his descendants was the coming of One who would be that ladder to unite earth and heaven, Jew and Gentile, to unite as brothers those who had hated each other as enemies.

The Messiah-Jesus is the only adequate answer to the human need of a spiritual ladder. He was set up on earth like Jacob's ladder. He was the seed of Abraham and seed of David; he was circumcised and kept the Law.

The Jesus-ladder was made of durable material. He was holy, harmless, undefiled, separate from sinners. He was the only One who could say, "Which of you convinceth me of sin?" Even Pilate, the judge who condemned him, had to say, "I find no fault in him." He was the only one who could ever say, "Come unto me all you that labor and are heavy laden and I will give you rest."

Century after century has found its hosts of Jews and Gentiles who have come to the Messiah of Israel and found entrance to the presence of God.

The ladder that Jacob saw is still standing.

So what is EASTER?

Maybe it has to do with Bunnies and Bonnets... but it doesn't have ANYTHING to do with JESUS.

Maybe you find it easy to believe in a bunny that hippity-hops around in new clothes, lays eggs, and croons about a parade on 5TH AVENUE...

But, we Jews, well, we just don't BUY it.

The word EASTER is only found ONCE in the New Testament,* and even then it's a mistranslation of the word

חֶסַ or

πάσχα

which is PESACH or PASCHA.

And if you ask any Hebrew or Greek, they will tell you that it doesn't mean

EASTER, it means PASSOVER!

*ACTS 12:4

Now, some of us Jews
<u>do</u> know that Jesus is the
 Promised
MESSIAH
 <u>and</u> that He died for
<u>our</u> sins & rose
  again
   from the dead...

  <u>AND</u> that HE IS
  <u>RETURNING</u>
   AGAIN!!!

 But we don't want to
 celebrate <u>a</u> holiday that's
 called EASTER
 because that's the name
 of a Gentile goddess who
 was supposed to have gone
 to hell... and stayed there.

 <u>So</u> why hunt around for a
 bunch of rotten EGGS?!

FORGET ABOUT
Bunnies and
~~~~~ ~~~~
        BONNETS
and the insipid
FOLDEROL!!!!!!

Join us in knowing
    that Jesus,
    the Jewish Messiah,
    has given EVERYONE
    a reason-to Celebrate.
       ~~~~~

So REJOICE,
   BE GLAD,
HALLELUJAH!

    and a happy Passover
       to our Christian &
       Jewish friends.

Christianity Has Not Failed; It Has Not Been Tried

By RUSSELL KIRK

Since the Messiah Jesus was born at Bethlehem, nearly two thousand years have elapsed—and yet God's kingdom has not been established upon earth. As G. K. Chesterton wrote, "Christianity has not failed; it has not been tried."

The precepts of Jesus, expressed often in parable, from the first were imperfectly understood by many; for those who did apprehend the teaching, still the way was hard.

The Christian Church itself often had come to honor the letter of Jesus' precepts more than the spirit. It is not surprising that Christian teaching did not succeed in erasing human vices; the surprising thing is the degree to which that faith has enabled many people to order their souls, and so to improve the order of the commonwealth.

The kingdom of which Jesus spoke was the kingdom of love, not of a novel political domination. Jesus accepted the existing political structures of the world, saying that men should render unto Caesar what was Caesar's and to

God what was God's. In all his preaching there was no advocacy of a political and social revolution, nor any plan for new social organization.

He said nothing about war; he did not denounce slavery. The establishment of justice must come through the waking of minds and souls, not through armed force. Jesus came to save sinners: to rouse them to righteousness. He worked upon consciences, and those consciences worked as best they could to redeem society from its vices and brutalities.

How was it that a religion so austere and exacting, so insistent upon charity and chastity, so contemptuous of worldly goods, seeming so impractical, won over the masses of the ancient world? Many other religions, asking less of their votaries and apparently offering more to human appetites, competed with Christianity at its beginning. Yet Christian faith increased among all social classes, while the other forms of worship withered away.

One reason for this triumph was Jesus' burning concern for the poor. By that word he did not mean the destitute, but rather the humble, the meek, the powerless, the oppressed—those who submitted themselves to the will of God. In that sense, the vast majority of people in the Roman imperial system were poor; in that sense, the vast majority of people in the 20th-century world remain poor. Those powerless ones heard the words that were preached for them—at first in the cities, presently in the countryside.

Most of all, the new faith taught people how to restore harmony in their souls in this earthly life; and it offered them the promise of the life eternal. Through many pagan cults, the people of the Roman world in imperial times sought after personal immortality. But the mysteries of those cults were unconvincing; while the life eternal, as preached through the world by Jesus' apostles, seemed to many men more real than the decaying society about them. What had begun among a handful of Jews in Galilee became the hope of life everlasting for the many millions of the Roman Empire.

Some tell us nowadays that we live in the "post-Christian era." Yet our time is very like, in many respects, the age to which Saul-Paul of Tarsus preached the word of Jesus. God is the loving father of all, Paul told the infant communities of Christians; only through Him may man be saved from the wages of sin. But man has alienated himself from God by idolatry, by forbidden sensuality, by injustice. Through repentance and obedience, and the operation of God's grace, redemption is possible.

Man by himself, said Paul, is too feeble to offer atonement for sin. It is redemption through the Messiah Jesus that enables man to escape from a state of sin. Physical lusts are bound up with this power of sin, but are only one aspect or consequence of mankind's separation from God.

The real root of sin is what we now call egoism: the desire of the individual to usurp the throne of God, to defy the Father, to pretend that the Father does not exist. The life eternal means that the human person continues to exist as a soul, in harmony with God but not absorbed. Beyond the jaws of death, we are promised the resurrection of the body. Were it not true that he should escape from death and live forever in Christ, said Paul, he would be the most miserable of men.

What among the classical philosophers had been only a dim surmise and longing, became in Christianity a confident dogma. Whatever its commercial trappings nowadays, the joyous festival of Christmas celebrates the redeeming of mankind, through the atonement of the Messiah Jesus for all human sins.

god was
mourning
over the dead,
the persecuted,
those whose minds
were scrambled with the
lust for power.

god was
suffering
along with every
humiliation and
each act of violence.

god was
weeping
over the lost souls
who were hurled
namelessly
into cold eternity.

Why did God just
sit back and let
it happen?
WHY DIDN'T **he**
STOP IT?

why?

The answer to this is not snappy nor is it smuggly self-satisfied. It is hard to explain and hard to understand. It has to do with love that is really **love.**

GOD made man to be loved by Him and to be able to give love in return.

Love must always be a choice.

GOD created man to have the power to choose Love, to choose peace, to choose humility and righteousness...

...but man has chosen
hatred, war and pride.

GOD mourns over our poor choices, but HE
will never violate our
right
to decide.

In the world
that we, mankind,
have collectively
chosen to live in,
it was a set of
historical decisions
that permitted the
Third Reich to grow
and prosper. Decisions
to "play dumb"
to "not care"...
decisions to look
upon the misery of
fellow human beings
as
"somebody else's
business"
and not our own.

Like Cain we
have shrugged
and retorted,
am I my
brother's
keeper?

we *have responded to the privilege of decision-making with a timeline full of irresponsible choices.*

And <u>we</u> ask,

where was GOD?

HE WAS WATCHING
        AND WEEPING.

GOD is watching & weeping &
suffering & mourning
for <u>us</u> still...
                even
                now.
                TODAY.

Yozel's Hasid

By J. FELDMAN

The Pletzel in Paris is a quarter thickly settled with Jews. Though only a few hundred feet from the famous Place de la Bastile, it is here that one can meet many of the types and characters immortalized by Sholom Aleichem. Rabbis, dayonim* and slaughterers often engage in heated discussions about kashruth,* divorce, marriages, and other topics, and the atmosphere is reminiscent of shtetl* life of years ago.

The Pletzel, like other close communities, has its peculiar, slightly different people, and the one whom I was privileged to meet was not an ordinary fellow.

Yozel's Hasid

Picture now a Jew with beard and side-locks, long kaftan,* with a broad talith-katan,* and a prayer shawl sack in which, in addition to the prayer shawl, are two pairs of phylacteries.* As is customary among the Hasidim,* close up to the talith and the phylacteries are a Pentateuch* and—would you believe it— a New Testament in a Hebrew translation.

You are astounded? Yet it was a fact. Such a Jew lived in Paris, and Jews knew him as they knew a bad penny. Twice a day he went to synagogue to pray, and he prayed with fervor, with swayings and gesticulations. He observed all the Jewish customs, yet he also believed that Jesus was the Messiah.

He believed that Jesus was a prophet who came to redeem his people and the whole world, but that he was misunderstood and crucified. He believed with his whole heart that as soon as we Jews accept Jesus as the Messiah, then the world would cease to taunt us and respect us as the chosen people.

He came to Paris shortly before World War I, back in 1914, and was very pious, a hasid of the famous Rebbe of Ger. And so he lived in the Pletzel, supported by his son, a wealthy man, and all day long he prayed and studied and steeped himself in piety.

Suddenly, in the year 1920, missionaries came into the area and conducted street meetings. The old man became incensed, but finally his curiosity got the better of him and he plucked up courage and listened to what they had to say. Several times after that he went to hear them, and returned home with some of their literature in Yiddish and Hebrew.

Since then people said that a demon took possession of him. He became an ardent believer that Jesus was the Messiah.

At first he preached in the synagogue that Jews should accept Jesus, and pointed out passages from the Tenach* to prove his statements.

It created a great scandal. Jews shouted: "Transgressor of Israel, go to a church and be baptized. What do you want in a synagogue?"

He was thrown out of one synagogue after another until he stopped preaching about Jesus. Finally he shut himself up, talked to no one, only went to synagogue, said his prayers, and went home.

Jews smiled when they saw him, and when he swayed during his prayers they said, "See how Yozel's hasid is swaying and gesticulating. Soon he will go home to kiss the cross and learn several chapters out of Jesus' Torah."

All sorts of stories circulated about him. Some said that he wore a cross on his breast. Others said that he carried with him a picture of Jesus, and, during the evening prayer when no one was about, he kissed the picture. But his son, with whom I talked, said these stories were not true.

I was curious about the man, and went to the home several times, but did not find him in. At last I was rewarded. I found him sitting in his room, but had difficulty in drawing him into conversation. At last he spoke:

"What can I say to you about matters of faith? You perhaps do not believe in anything, possibly not even in God!"

Then, having broken his silence, he began to complain of the unbelieving world which does not believe in God because it cannot see Him, and yet accepts such things as Einstein's theory of relativity even though they admit that they do not understand it.

I explained that I was curious to learn how he, a pious Jew, came to believe in Jesus. He washed his hands, straightened his yarmulke,* and with heat and fire began: "Who then should believe in him—the gentiles? The wonder is that a gentile should believe in him at all, in him who said to turn the other cheek when you are struck!"

He said that only Jews can truly accept belief in Jesus as the Messiah and regard him as the last Prophet, for gentiles can never accept such a lofty faith. It is next to impossible for them to walk in his ways, for first of all, Yeshua, as he called him, commanded to observe all the Jewish laws, the entire Torah,* and gentiles do not even know this.

He spoke about passages from the Torah and the Prophets, and how Jesus came into the world to teach all men the way of God. Then, with a deep sigh, he said, "Well, I have babbled enough. It's time for me to turn to my studies."

74

His last words to me were, "Tell them, those simple-
tons, that 'Yozel's hasid,' as they call me, is not crazy as
they think. I have not become a goy,* but am a true, completed Jew."

I left him, but the figure of the old man with beard and
side-locks, "Yozel's hasid," stayed with me a long time.—
Translated from the New York Yiddish FORWARD.

דאָס געזאַנג
פֿון שמעון הצדיק

אַצינד טוסטו אָפּלאָזן דײַן קנעכט, אָ גאָט,
לויט דײַן װאָרט, בשָׁלום;
װאָרים מײַנע אויגן האָבן געזען דײַן ישׁועה,
װאָס דו האָסט אָנגעברייט פֿאַר אַלע פֿעלקער;
אַ ליכט צו באַלײַכטן די אומות,
און דער כָּבוד פֿון דײַן פֿאָלק יִשְׂרָאֵל.

די בשׂורה לויט לוקאַס ב': 29—32

75

This I Believe

By ADOLPH SAPHIR

A young Jew, by the grace of God, has been brought to believe in Jesus as his Saviour. From the Scriptures—from Moses and the prophets—he has found the Messiah promised to the fathers.

He believes that he is not saved by works, but by grace, through faith. He believes, as it is written of Abraham:

"Abraham believed God, and it was counted to him for righteousness" (Genesis 15:6), and as the Prophet Habakkuk declares, "The just shall live by faith" (Habakkuk 4:4).

He believes in *God the Father Almighty*, creator of heaven and earth, as it is written in Genesis 1:1:

"In the beginning God created the heavens and the earth."

He believes in *Jesus the Messiah* as he was promised to Abraham in Genesis 12:3:

"In your seed all the families of the earth will be blessed."

He believes that he will be the Shiloh of the tribe of Judah, to whom shall be the gathering of the nations, as announced in: Genesis 49:10; II Samuel 7:16; Isaiah 11; Ezekiel 37:25, and Hosea 3:5.

He believes that Jesus is the anointed one, the prince, who is to be cut off, but not for himself (Daniel 9:25, 26).

And as a Jew he believes that this Messiah was *conceived by the Holy Spirit*, and born of the Virgin Mary, as the Lord said by Isaiah in chapter 7, verse 14:

"Behold, a virgin shall conceive and bear a son, and shall call his name Immanuel."

And in Isaiah 9:6, the prophet rejoices: "To us a child is born, to us a son is given; and the government will be upon his shoulder, and his name will be called 'Wonderful Counselor, Mighty God, Everlasting Father, Prince of Peace."

And he believes the prediction by Micah in chapter 5, verse 1, that out of Bethlehem shall come forth one who is to be ruler in Israel, whose goings forth are from of old, even from everlasting.

And, according to the Tenach,* he believes that this Messiah was *a man of sorrows*, was wounded, bruised, and acquainted with grief (Isaiah 53:3-5); that he suffered under Pontius Pilate, as stated in Psalm 2:2: "The kings of the earth set themselves, and the rulers take counsel together against the Lord and his anointed."

And *He died and was buried* according to the prophecy of Isaiah: "He poured out his soul to death, and made his grave with the wicked" (chapter 53:12).

He *rose on the third day* as David said in Psalm 16, verse 10: "For thou wilt not leave my soul in hell, nor suffer thy holy One to see corruption;" and again, in the 118th Psalm: "The stone which the builders rejected has become the head of the corner. This is the Lord's doing; it is marvelous in our eyes."

Hosea, in the sixth chapter, predicted that on the third day God would revive us, and in the second chapter of Jonah the prophet prefigured who was three days in the belly of the fish, and then came forth, a sign of the power and grace of God.

And, as a Jew receiving the testimony of the prophets, he believes that the Messiah *ascended into heaven*, for David says in Psalm 110:1 "The Lord says to my lord: 'Sit at my right hand, till I make your enemies your footstool.'"

And he believes that Jesus *shall come again* with the clouds of heaven and in great glory, as Daniel beheld in the nightvision, chapter 7:13, 14:

"And behold, with the clouds of heaven there came one like a son of man, and he came to the Ancient of Days and was presented before him. And to him was given dominion and glory and kingdom, that all peoples, nations, and languages should serve him; his dominion is an everlasting dominion, which shall not pass away, and his kingdom one that shall not be destroyed.''

All this he believes concerning Jesus, the Messiah, on the authority of Moses and the prophets.

And on the same authority, as a Jew, he believes in the *Holy Spirit*, as it is recorded at the very threshold of the sacred volume, Genesis 1:2:

"The Spirit of God moved over the face of the waters.''

And the Prophets Joel and Ezekiel tell that the Lord will pour out His Spirit on all flesh, and Isaiah said: "I will pour out my Spirit upon your descendants'' (chapter 44:3).

The Prophet Zechariah described the Messiah as the Man whom we pierced, sending forth a Spirit of compassion and supplication upon the inhabitants of Jerusalem (chapter 12:10).

And he believes in *the communion of saints*, as signified by the chosen generation, the royal priesthood, a holy nation Exodus 19:6; Deuteronomy 14:2; 26:18).

He believes in *the forgiveness of sins*, as David described the blessedness of the man to whom the Lord imputes no iniquity, whose transgression is forgiven, whose sin is covered (Psalm 32: 1, 2).

And he believes in *the resurrection of the dead*, as it is written in Isaiah 26:19: "Thy dead shall live, their bodies shall rise;'' and in *life eternal* as David says in Psalm 16:11: "Thou dost show me the path of life; in thy presence there is fulness of joy, in thy right hand are pleasures for evermore.''

This is, by the grace of God, his faith, founded on the declarations of Moses and the prophets, and held by him as a Jew, a son of Abraham. And, like that early disciple, having found in Jesus of Nazareth the Messiah, he exclaims: "Rabbi, you are the Son of God! You are the King of Israel'' (John 1:49).

"*Joy Cometh in the Morning*"

The question uppermost in my mind was: What was the meaning of the long nightmare for our people? Was the holocaust all in vain? This could not be since I had so many tokens of God's presence and intervention in my own life and in the history of my people. Was it for the punishment of our sins? But did the poverty-stricken Jews in Poland commit more sins than the almost godless and affluent Jews of the West? Yet they were saved.

Perhaps the western Jews were saved from physical death not because of their own merits, but because of western Christianity which was less degenerate than ours in the East. In the West the Christians practiced what they preached, and were ready to fight and die, not only for their country, but to save the remnant of Jews in Europe.

If my people had known the things that pertain to their salvation, namely, to believe in Jesus as their Messiah and to proclaim him to the people in Poland and the rest of Eastern Europe, this disaster would never have happened.

Yet there was fruit from the blood of the Jewish martyrs. There was the national and physical revival of Israel. The Lord had permitted Israel to be smitten by the heathen, and now he offered the hand of reconciliation through the Gentiles. It was as if the nations suddenly realized that they had exceeded the measure of their wickedness towards our people, and in repentance voted a home for Israel in her own land. Thus they contributed to the fulfillment of prophecies which speak of Israel's return to her borders, as it is written in Deuteronomy 30:4: "If your outcasts are in the uttermost parts of heaven, from there the Lord your God will bring you into the land which your fathers possessed, that you may possess it."

There must also be a spiritual significance to all these things that had happened, and I was reminded of words in Romans 2:4:"Or do you presume upon the riches of his kindness and forbearance and patience? Do you not know that God's kindness is meant to lead you to repentance?"

Perhaps God is now dealing with Israel in the same manner. First by severity and sufferings, and now by his goodness. He is encouraging the Gentile nations to help Israel regather the Jewish dispersion to her own land.

Though Israel has greatly expanded her boundaries, the majority of the Jewish people still prefer to live outside of the promised land. Yet Israel is where Jewish history began, and where, according to God's Word, it will be consummated.

Out of the pain and throes of World War II, the State of Israel came into being. The hope of Israel to be "a light to the Gentiles" has not materialized, Many previously friendly Gentiles have been disappointed with Israel's failure to provide compensation to Arab refugees whose possessions

Israel took over, and with her failure to give full religious liberty and accept under the Law of Return those of our people who call themselves "Hebrew Christians."

The only "light to the Gentiles" is still Jesus the Messiah, who is also part of the Jewish people. He is "the glory of his people Israel." One day Israel will also partake of this light and glory, and then Israel's dream to be a light to the nations will be fulfilled.

How shall these things happen, and when? The Hebrew Scriptures give us a clear answer in Zechariah 12:10: "And I will pour out on the house of David and the inhabitants of Jerusalem a spirit of compassion and supplication, so that they shall look on him whom they have pierced."

Saul-Paul, student of Rabbi Gamaliel, describes this time in Romans 11:26: "And so all Israel shall be saved; as it is written, The Deliverer will come from Zion, he will banish ungodliness from Jacob."

In that day our people will become a light to the whole world. Only then will we fulfill our age-long spiritual dream, as recorded in Zechariah 8:23: "Thus says the Lord of hosts: In those days ten men from the nations of every tongue shall take hold of the robe of a Jew, saying, 'Let us go with you, for we have heard that God is with you.'"

What a wonderful future to look forward to! I am confident that this was the night before the Light will break for Israel, and through her to the whole world.

In Psalm 30, verse 5, we read: "For his anger is but for a moment, and his favor is for a lifetime. Weeping may tarry for the night, but joy comes with the morning."

כִּי רֶגַע בְּאַפּוֹ חַיִּים

בִּרְצוֹנוֹ בָּעֶרֶב יָלִין בֶּכִי וְלַבֹּקֶר רִנָּה׃

Who's Who

Lord Beaconsfield

Better known as Benjamin Disraeli, was not only an outstanding man of letters, but also one of England's great statesmen. While Prime Minister he made Queen Victoria Empress of India, and obtained for Britain controlling interest in the Suez Canal.

An ardent champion of the rights of his people during the period of their disfranchisement, the Jewish Encyclopedia, Vol. IV, p. 620, declares:

"Disraeli did not plead for toleration, but for the admission of Jews to full privileges on account of their special merit."

In his biography of Lord Bentinck, p. 363, Disraeli asserts:

"Christians may continue to persecute Jews and Jews may persist in disbelieving Christians, but who can deny that Jesus of Nazareth, the Incarnate Son of the Most High God, is the eternal glory of the Jewish race?" *See page* 54

Alfred Edersheim

Born in Vienna, brought up in Budapest, Hungary, he received a thorough Jewish and secular education. During his student days he was so influenced by the teachings of the New Testament that he not only accepted Jesus as his Messiah, but dedicated his life to His service.

Dr. Edersheim is best known as a theological author and lecturer at the University of Oxford, where he held the position of Grinfield Lecturer on the Septuagint.

He was a voluminous writer, and his LIFE AND TIMES OF JESUS THE MESSIAH is considered the finest of its kind in the English language. *See page* 5

Nine miles west of the river Bug, four miles southeast of Chelm, in the Lublin district of Poland, was the village home of Rachmiel Frydland.

The parents were religious Jews, and at an early age Rachmiel's studies began. Being an avid student, he progressed to studies in Rashi,* then on to the Talmud,* and finally Yeshivah* studies in Warsaw.

While in the Yeshivah he became disatisfied, and began to drift away from Rabbinical Judaism. Since less time was spent on Talmud, more time was spent on the study of the Tenach,* the straight forward words of Scripture. Finally he left the Yeshivah, never to return.

Needing lodging, Rachmiel found a room with a tailor and his wife who liked to go to the "missionaries." They invited him to go with them so he could tell whether or not the Bible said that Jesus was the Messiah. This appealed to his pride, and so he went.

Contact with Jews who believed, reading the New Testament, questions and answers, much prayer on the part of many people, including himself, helped Rachmiel finally realize for certain that Jesus was his personal Saviour, his Messiah.

The world situation was becoming dark. Hitler had become ruler of Germany in 1933, and by September 1939, bombs began to fall in Warsaw. The Polish population looked for a scapegoat, and after the surrender of Warsaw to the Nazis, life in the city became unbearable for Jews. 1939 to 1942 were years of great danger: humiliation, starvation, physical assault, commandeered slave labor, and finally Hitler's plan of complete extermination of the Jews.

Rachmiel lived the life of a hunted animal. Betrayed by Polish townspeople, befriended by a few, rejected by the pastor of his church, helped by another, a change in identity, spending one night here, the next somewhere else, sleeping in a coffin at an undertaking establishment, Rachmiel came to the point where he wanted to die.

It was then that Rachmiel decided to stay with his people in the Warsaw ghetto, knowing that there would be no escape. But the hand of God interfered, and he was persuaded to again take his chance on the outside so he might be a spokesman for the doomed Jewish Christians. Shortly thereafter the ghetto was burned, and more than 5,000 Jews were killed.

A most unforgettable day was the seventh anniversary of his baptism, January 15, 1945, when the German army was defeated, and Polish and Soviet troops entered Warsaw. The war was over.

A life of hardship, tragedy, uncertainties, rejection, abuse, never caused Rachmiel Frydland to waver in his faith. His story is beautifully told in his booklet, "Joy Cometh in the Morning." See page 79

Erich Hoffer

A manual laborer all his life, and for twenty-five years a San Francisco longshoreman, Mr. Hoffer was a self-educated historian, philosopher, and author of a number of books including: "The True Believer," "The Ordeal of Change," and "The Temper of Our Time."

Mr. Hoffer has appeared on television and presented his views on such topics as civil rights, the urban crisis, law and order, the younger generation, religion and death. He has also been teaching at the University of California at Berkeley. See page 16

Fred Kendal

The son of a Russian Jew and her second husband, Fred was reared in an atmosphere of love and devotion. His mother, Esther, accepted Jesus as her Messiah through her first husband, Julius Finestone, and was the mother of three children.

Upon the death of Julius, Esther married William Kendal, and they were the parents of Fred and his sister Emma.

Though born in London, Fred's earliest memories are of Toronto, Canada, where his parents witnessed to their fellow Jews by word and deed.

Fred caught the pioneering spirit from his parents, and after finishing his education founded the Canadian Baptist Testimony to the Jews which he headed until he went to Detroit in 1934. Continuing there for many years he founded and established Israel's Remnant, and in 1957 opened a branch in Brookline, Massachusetts.

Through his writings, visitation, counseling, participation in conferences and seminars, as well as Bible exposition, Fred Kendal was a radiant witness for the Messiah Jesus. *See page 56*

Russell Kirk

Described by both TIME and NEWSWEEK as one of America's leading thinkers, Dr. Kirk is also the author of eighteen books and of several hundred periodical essays, short stories, and long reviews.

Dr. Kirk, whose syndicated column is distributed by the Los Angeles TIMES Syndicate and is published in more than a hundred daily newspapers, not only writes, but speaks on political thought, educational theory, literary criticism, foreign affairs, moral questions, and many other themes.

His latest book, "Eliot and His Age," published by Random House, has been highly acclaimed. *See page 64*

Max Reich

The son of Orthodox Jewish parents, Max Reich was born in Berlin, Germany, and from early childhood was steeped in the traditions which his family carried over from their forebears, the Sephardic Jews of medieval Spain.

At the death of his mother, the boy was sent to England

where he was schooled in the meticulous observance of Jewish law. Shy and sensitive, he early turned to the Scriptures, particularly the Psalms, where he was much influenced by the portrayal of God as a Redeemer, Shepherd, Healer, Friend, Rock, Refuge,

Out of curiosity the young man attended a meeting of the Salvation Army, and it was an unforgettable experience which led to much soul searching, and finally to an acceptance of Jesus as his Messiah.

Of this experience he wrote: "I did not imagine that I had left my religion. I had found it, discovered its true meaning. I felt perfectly at home in my discovery that Jesus was the completion and fulfillment of all that was best and holiest and highest in the faith of my beloved people."

Max Reich was a popular and much loved teacher and lecturer, and his interpretations of the Psalms, and his profound understanding of Messianic prophecy brought him into touch with thousands of people.

Throughout his life Max Reich was a prolific writer, and his works include meditations, spiritually penetrating essays, studies in the Psalms, and poetry. He has been aptly called, "The Sweet Singer of Israel." See page 20

Moishe Rosen

Whose name is synonymous with "Jews for Jesus," was born in Denver, and reared in a more or less secular Jewish home. While in college he was a convinced agnostic. His girl friend was raised Orthodox, but became a militant atheist. After their marriage Moishe continued to observe some of the old traditions, but religious differences were not too important.

Independent of each other they came to grips with the claims of Jesus as the Messiah, Ceil first, and then Moishe.

For several years now the home base for Moishe is in the San Francisco Bay area, though he travels the length and breadth of the country. In his words:

"We are like a family group. What is different with us is that we preach to everyone the good news that the Messiah came, atoned for our sins, rose from the grave, and is coming again. We've seen young people and some older ones too become, literally, transformed.

"We don't think of ourselves as Jesus Freaks, although we've been called that. We're trying to be part of the Jewish community and be involved—to support the community as much as they will let us.

"Some rabbis say we're apostates who have thrown away our rights as Jews. Our answer is that we have become completed Jews by accepting the Messiah as the final, once-and-for-all atonement for our sins. We observe the Jewish holidays and traditional family ceremonies, and do all we can to preserve our Jewish identity.

"We know who we are. We are Jews who belong to the family of God through faith in the Messiah Jesus. We invite other Jews to join us in this beautiful adventure."

See page 33

Adolph Saphir

The Saphir family was well known in Hungary, and greatly respected. The grandfather of Adolph was learned in the Jewish law, and had much influence among his co-religionists. His uncle Moritz was recognized as one of the great literary men of the period, and his father Israel was a merchant, a Hebrew scholar, and had a knowledge of German, French, and English literature. He was also interested in philosophical and theological studies, and rendered much service to the cause of education in Hungary.

Adolph began his formal education at the age of four, and was considered quite a genius. At the age of eight he wrote German poems, and when eleven passed examinations to attend the University.

Both father and son became interested in the question of the Messiahship of Jesus, and Israel, after much thought, said: "It is very hard to give up in old age opinions cherished from youth and never doubted."

Nevertheless, Israel and his son Adolph became convinced, and never hesitated as to the course to be taken. At the age of sixty-three, when Adolph was twelve years old, they publicly professed their faith, which was shared by other members of the immediate family.

After completing his undergraduate education at the University of Glasgow, he went on to Edinburgh to pursue his studies in theology. He had great literary talent, not only as an imaginative writer, but also as a teacher. He had a wonderful power of compressing in short space a large and comprehensive view of his subject, and his fervency and thrilling method of delivery, plus his great knowledge of Scripture commanded much respect.

It has been said that Adolph Saphir knew and handled Old Testament Scripture as perhaps only a son of Abraham could. Moses and the Psalmists and the Prophets were his familiar friends and intimates, and he stressed the importance of viewing Scripture in relation to the Messiah of Israel, the Redeemer of God's people.

He was a noted preacher, expositor of Scripture, writer, and his life was given over to proclaiming that the Old Testament and the New are one. *See page* 76

GLOSSARY

Dayonim: judges of religious matters

Eretz Israel: Land of Israel

Goy: Hebrew term commonly applied to a non-Jew

Haggadah: ritual recited in the home on the first evening of Passover

Hasidim: Jewish sect characterized by its emphasis on mysticism, prayer, religious zeal and joy

Kaftan: long garment with long sleeves and tied at the waist by a girdle

Kashruth: ritual lawfulness, especially of food

Pentateuch: Greek term for the five books of Moses, known in Jewish tradition as "The Written Law"

Phylacteries: two black leather boxes fastened to leather straps, containing four portions of the Pentateuch written on parchment, and bound on the arm and head and worn on weekdays during morning prayer

Rashi: abbreviated name of Rabbi Solomon Yitzhaki, or Ben Isaac, author of the most popular commentary on the Bible and the Talmud

Shavuot: the Feast of Weeks, also known as Pentecost, observed fifty days after the second day of Passover as the Festival of the First-Fruits. After the destruction of the Temple, Shavuot commemorates the giving of the Ten Commandments by God to Moses on Mt. Sinai

Shtetl: a small town

Talith-Katan: small prayer shawl

Talmud: compilation of Jewish law and tradition, consisting of the Mishnah and the Gemara, and being either the edition produced in Palestine, also known as the Jerusalem Talmud, or the larger, more important one, the Babylonian Talmud

Tenach: the Bible made up of the Pentateuch (the five books of Moses), the Neviim (Prophets), and Ketuvim (Writings)

Torah: traditionally given to Moses at Sinai and, in a larger sense, includes both the Written and the Oral Law, the entire talmudic literature and commentaries

Yarmulke: skullcap worn for prayers, and, by religious Jews, at all times

Yeshivah: Jewish traditional school devoted primarily to the study of the Talmud and rabbinic literature

OTHER PUBLICATIONS

The New Testament in Yiddish
The Good News According to Matthew
The Man with the Book
Would I? Would You?
Raisins and Almonds
A Way in the Wilderness
Gospel of Matthew in Yiddish